Original title:
Earrings in the Twilight

Copyright © 2025 Creative Arts Management OÜ
All rights reserved.

Author: Olivia Sterling
ISBN HARDBACK: 978-1-80586-014-3
ISBN PAPERBACK: 978-1-80586-486-8

Celestial Lure

In the sky, a wink from afar,
Bouncing light like a shooting star.
A cat with jewels in her ear,
Prances like she has no fear.

Stars giggle, they twinkle with glee,
As squirrels spar in a wild spree.
The moon plays tag, oh what a sight,
While crickets hum a tune of delight.

Glittering Reveries

Sparkles twinkle, making claims,
On the waltz of silly games.
A squirrel wears a set of rings,
And laughs as if he's king of bling.

Boys with bows and shiny ties,
Trade their dreams for golden pies.
While shadows blend and giggle loud,
Twilight dances, feeling proud.

The Allure of Darkness

In the evening's tricky glow,
Bouncing shadows steal the show.
Tiny giggles fill the air,
As lost socks dance without a care.

Mismatched pairs in playful flight,
Whirling under stars so bright.
The moon whispers cheeky tunes,
While cats plot heists beneath the dunes.

Whispered Secrets of the Night

In the dark, secrets take flight,
With owls gossiping, quite the sight.
A hedgehog wearing a glow-in-the-dark,
Thought it was fashion, but missed the mark!

The shadows dance in a silly spree,
With words they chuckle, oh so free.
The night holds laughter like sassy sprites,
Chasing away the mundane sights.

Night's Glimmering Journey

A raccoon dons a sparkly crown,
While chasing shadows all around.
Fireflies flash like tiny beads,
As the night sprinkles laughter, indeed!

Bats in shades of polka dots,
Fly by, forget their fancy spots.
The breeze tells jokes, I swear it's true,
As every branch sways and breaks in two.

A Canvas of Light

Brushes mix a splash of fun,
As stars begin their nightly run.
A daisy headband on a hound,
Makes laughter echo all around.

Moonbeams paint the world so bright,
Creating chaos in the night.
With every giggle, colors bloom,
As shadows wiggle in their room.

Nocturnal Brilliance

The night wears spectacles of glee,
As owls hoot tales of jubilee.
Fireflies blink with silly wit,
While crickets join in for the bit.

A raccoon dons a shiny hat,
And pets applaud this silly spat.
In the glow of a raucous scene,
The whimsical chime of a diamond dream.

Shadows of Silver

In the evening's gentle sway,
A mouse wore pearls, ready to play,
He danced in circles, round and round,
While cats just blinked, lost and found.

A squirrel sighed, with jesting pride,
Clipped acorns shiny, pinned aside,
He twirled with tricks, in twilight's gleam,
Making all of nature beam.

Dance of the Diminishing Light

As shadows shrink in evening's grasp,
A glowworm gave a twinkly gasp,
While frogs croaked jests in mirrored lakes,
Beneath the stars, a chorus breaks.

A rabbit hopped in dotted lanes,
With carrot crowns on fuzzy brains,
His friends all giggled, light a-flick,
In dusky fun, they danced real quick.

Twinkling Secrets

Fireflies flashed their secrets bright,
In moonlit games, they took to flight,
A hidden treasure up the tree,
Was just a snack—a honey bee!

The owls laughed low, in between hoots,
While spiders wore the finest suits,
Every twig became a stage,
In nature's play, they turned the page.

Luminous Lullabies

In the gloaming glow of day,
Crickets sung in their breezy way,
A lullaby to wind and leaf,
With rhythms light, and never grief.

The fox wore shades of golden hue,
In twilight's cloak, he hopscotched too,
With every leap, he snagged a grin,
Who knew that dusk could bring such spin?

Velvet Whispers of Dusk

In shadows soft, a joke takes flight,
A pair of jewels, not quite in sight.
They dangle low, like fish on a hook,
And giggles echo 'round every nook.

A sparkle here, a wink of mirth,
The night unfolds, giving birth.
To laughter shared, oh what a sight,
With bling that twinkles in fading light.

The Allure of Midnight Baubles

Midnight charms that sway and sing,
With every step, they dance and cling.
A snicker comes from a nearby cat,
As if to say, 'Aren't they quite fat?'

Down the hall, they spin around,
In a game with shadows, lost then found.
Who knew that jewels could wink so sly,
As frolicsome clouds drift by in the sky?

Glimmering Reflections of Twilight Dreams

Glints and gleams in a playful breeze,
As friends poke fun at their own unease.
They flop and jingle, causing a scene,
Like goats in a pasture, wild and keen.

A twirl, a flip, and a cheeky grin,
As color fights with the day's dim spin.
With laughter entwined, they spin in glee,
Dreaming of what this night could be.

Shadows and Sparkles at Day's End

Underneath the moon's soft beam,
A treasure hunt, or so it seems.
Lost in jest, they plot and plan,
While sparkles twirl, like a lively fan.

A dash of humor, a splash of gold,
In the dim light, stories unfold.
With each chuckle, they dance with flair,
As shadows stretch, no worry or care.

Twilight's Hidden Treasure

In the dusk, a sparkle shines,
A squirrel dons some shiny finds.
Chasing shadows, it missteps,
Ends up stuck in fancy webs.

A raccoon wears a golden chain,
Strutting down the lane, quite vain.
But every heist comes with a cost,
Now he's learned his flair is lost.

The moonlight winks, a playful tease,
As cats parade with utmost ease.
With strange adornments on their heads,
They strut and purr, in jeweled threads.

So twilight brings a joyful laugh,
In the park, the critters half.
Gems are lost, but fun is found,
In this treasure town, they bound.

Enigmatic Allures

A snail in pearls glides down the way,
Looking fancy, come what may.
It slows the pace, to catch a glance,
Painting trails with a jeweled dance.

A grasshopper hops, with style so neat,
Wearing boots of glitter on its feet.
It trips on blades, a raucous show,
As crickets laugh at the wild flow.

Under stars, the creatures plot,
To fashion bling from what they've got.
A ladybug with a fancy hat,
Steals the spotlight; imagine that!

As twilight falls, laughter rings,
In this world of oddball things.
Adornments flit in every spot,
And all are treasures—believe it or not!

Twilight's Gleaming Veil

At dusk, come creatures with a flair,
Draped in garments, threadbare rare.
A hedgehog dons a silver ring,
While croaking frogs begin to sing.

A firefly glows, a disco light,
Flashing bright in the soft night.
Bumbles are dressed in neon hues,
Stumbling 'round in their fancy shoes.

With every twirl and every slide,
The woodland critters take great pride.
A bear in sunglasses takes a bow,
Proclaiming, "Check me out, wow wow!"

The woodland folk unite in fun,
As twilight winks, the day is done.
In this playful, sparkly quest,
Even trouble's just a jest!

Mysterious Reflections

In the twilight, reflections gleam,
Creatures dance in a glossy dream.
A gopher dons a gold mustache,
Crawling slick with a hilarious dash.

The shadows laugh at the comical sight,
As owls hoot with pure delight.
A raccoon's disco, quite absurd,
Where every spot's a dance floor stirred.

With a bounce, a frog leaps high,
Wearing glasses that flip and fly.
It strikes a pose by the pond's glow,
As the queen of the night steals the show.

A party forms in the cool, dark air,
With every critter fashioning flair.
Whimsical styles twinkling bright,
In the secrets of the sly twilight.

Mystique of Soft Shimmer

In the evening glow they sway,
Like little jokes on holiday.
Twinkling, dancing on a whim,
They tease the night, they twist and brim.

A funny flair, a jester's play,
In shadows where the whispers stay.
Glimmers giggle, shadows jest,
A shimmering quiz, a fashion test.

They catch the moon, a cheeky grin,
Somersaulting, playful spin.
Whispers echo, laughter bright,
A sparkle party in the night.

Who knew such fun could dangle free?
A sparkly riddle, a sight to see.
In twilight's trick, they mock the fray,
A shimmering joke that won't decay.

Glistening Mosaic

Fragments of laughter, bright and bold,
Each piece a story, silly, untold.
They dangle low, they zip and zoom,
A dazzling dance in the mellow gloom.

With each bright twinkle, a chuckle flows,
A painted smile where the twilight glows.
Colors collide in a cheeky spree,
Glistening tales of hilarity.

They spin like tops, they hop and skip,
A playful crew on a nightly trip.
In the evening's grip, they whirl and twirl,
A mosaic of giggles, a joyful swirl.

So gather 'round, let laughter rise,
Under the stars, hear the goofy cries.
With every glimmer, a wink, a jest,
A glittering riot, we're truly blessed.

Hues of Enchantment

In the dusk, hues start to tease,
Colors flair, with a touch of breeze.
A playful twinkle, beneath the sun,
In tales of folly, they have their fun.

Winks of purple, blue, and gold,
Each shade a prank, vivid and bold.
Who knew colors could be so sly?
Hues of enchantment, oh my, oh my!

They mingle well, like pals in tow,
Under the starlight's gentle glow.
A palette of giggles, a chromatic jest,
Laughing together, we are all blessed.

As dusk falls down with a funny hue,
Colors giggle, just like me and you.
In every shade, a story they spin,
Creating joy, where laughter begins.

Celestial Charms

Stars are whispering, secrets glow,
With charms that jingle, to and fro.
A cosmic dance, a light-hearted spree,
Where the twinkling laughs, oh so free.

Each little charm has jokes to share,
In the cool twilight, they float in the air.
They tease the night, a cheeky sight,
A symphony of laughter, pure delight.

Amongst the planets, a merry crew,
Crafting tales that are silly and true.
With every glimmer, a giggly charm,
Safety in laughter, no cause for alarm.

So gaze above, let joy take flight,
With celestial charms in the night.
A cosmic giggle, bright and clear,
Where every twinkle brings us near.

Veils of Mystery

In the dark, they dance and sway,
Hiding secrets, come what may.
Each twist and turn, a funny twist,
A game of peek, none can resist.

They jingle lightly on a whim,
Like tiny bells on a playful limb.
Who knew charms could cause such cheer?
They wink and nod, 'Come closer, dear!'

The shadows laugh, a mischievous tune,
While daydreams float like a balloon.
A spark of joy around we flit,
With giggles borne from silly wit.

Dusk's Glimmering Gifts

As night falls down, the sparkles play,
Falling stars in a curious ballet.
Laughter echoes, they twist and turn,
Who knew shiny could make hearts yearn?

They dangle low from lobes of fun,
Making moments weigh a ton.
Oh, how they shine, the jesters bold,
In whispers sweet, their stories told.

With every toss of hair and cheek,
They beam with promise, oh-so-cheek!
Not just for looks, but for a laugh,
Creating tales, their dainty craft.

Midnight Sparkle

At midnight's peek, they come alive,
With glints of joy, they dive and thrive.
A twinkling race around the moon,
Like fireflies dancing all in tune.

In corners dark, they giggle bright,
Preparing for mischief, quite the sight!
With every bob and every sway,
They plot new schemes, come what may.

Tiny gems with cheeky winks,
Whispering tales in giggling blinks.
A rally cry for laughter's sake,
They sparkle, shine, and never break!

Twilight's Secret Vows

As twilight sets the sky aglow,
A lively charm begins to flow.
With secrets swayed in playful tones,
They tease the night with joyful moans.

Promises whispered in soft delight,
Turn the mundane into pure flight.
They sway between giggles and sighs,
With comfort found in friendly lies.

Like naughty sprites, they tease and twirl,
In a world spun of comedy's whirl.
Unraveling stories under starry skies,
They promise fun and sparkly highs.

Echoes of Elegance in Dim Light

In shadows they dangle, a sparkling tease,
A dance of delight in the gentle breeze.
They twirl like little hiccups of style,
Leaving giggles behind with every smile.

A shimmer in corners, where mischief resides,
Adventures await, on fashion's wild rides.
Oh, the tales they could tell, if only they spoke!
About how they startled the hapless bloke.

From flappers to hipsters, they've seen all the trends,
Sometimes a fashion error, but they make amends.
With a wink to the camera, they shine with glee,
As if whispering secrets: "Just wear us, be free!"

So here's to the gems in the ebb of the night,
With laughter their jewels become ever so bright.
In the echoing twilight, they giggle and play,
Creating a scene that just brightens the day.

Celestial Elegance in Dim Glow

A twinkle of mischief hangs close to the ear,
As if laughing at whispers that only they hear.
In this cosmic ballet, they sway with such grace,
Who knew that such humor could sparkle in place?

Mismatched and quirky, they dance with delight,
Like comets on the move in the soft velvet night.
Each jingle and jangle a chorus of cheer,
For the folks who dare to wear them, oh dear!

When the clock ticks on fashion and styles turn a page,
These playful pendants refuse to act their age.
They waddle and wobble with charm that's no lie,
A wink and a nod, they dare you to fly.

So toast to the style in this dim evening glow,
To the laughter, the joy, the glimmering show.
In a world of fine jewels, they're the fun-loving sprite,
Let's twirl and keep moving, hearts merry and light.

Glistening Essence of the Fading Day

At dusk they emerge, with a whimsical glint,
They've seen all the sillies, oh yes, they imprint.
Their shimmer a wink, their sparkle a laugh,
Such witty companions, they'll make you do math!

On shelves they may sit, quietly observing,
While quietly plotting, fun they'll be curving.
Each jangle a giggle, a soft, playful tease,
In the game of starlight, they aim to please.

A mishmash of colors, they hang with such flair,
The twilight can't help but stop and just stare.
They tease out the stories from every last glance,
As poets and dreamers begin their last dance.

So here's to the glimmer, the giggles they bring,
In the waning day's light, they twirl and they swing.
With laughter's embrace binding all in delight,
Their essence, a treasure, shining purely bright.

Twilight's Biography in Gemstone

In the fading daylight, they laugh and they glow,
Their antics and charm steal the evening show.
A memoir in glimmers, a playful parade,
Packed full of the mischief that twilight has made.

They tell juicy tales of awkward first dates,
Of people who tripped on their own fancy fates.
Like little guides for the giggly and bold,
In the history of jests, their sparkles are gold.

Wobbling and jingling, they join in the jest,
In the twilight's embrace, they are truly the best.
Every swing of their presence ignites a bright cheer,
As stars start to twinkle and bring joy ever near.

Raise a glass to the whimsy that dusk does bestow,
To the sparkling vibes that ebb, flow, and flow.
In the chronicles written of laughter and play,
These gems of the twilight forever will stay.

Silhouettes of Shine

In the glow of dusk, they dance,
A wobble here, a silly prance.
Reflecting stars, a comic show,
Who knew they'd steal the evening's glow?

With sparkles bobbing in playful glee,
They wink at shadows, wild and free.
A flailing laugh, a twinkle's fright,
Chasing the moon with all their might.

Oh, how they jiggle, oh, how they sway,
Mocking the night in a jesting display.
If laughter could glitter, they'd surely win,
Twisted in joy, let the fun begin!

So join the revel of silly delight,
As twinkling shapes take laughter to flight.
In the twilight's embrace, let's make a toast,
To glamorous antics, we love the most!

Gilded Sorrows

In a box of dreams, shiny and bright,
They giggle and whisper, from left to right.
Oh, what a tale, these baubles do weave,
Of mishaps and giggles, oh, please believe.

Lost one in soup, the other in tea,
A daring adventure, just wait and see!
Hearts skip a beat, the drama unfolds,
With laughter echoing, the story is told.

They tug at the lobes, with grace and with ease,
Teasing the sanity, oh, what a breeze!
A twist in the plot, who could have guessed?
These gilded sorrows, oh, they're the best!

So here's to the laughter that jingles and jives,
To the stories that sparkle and keep us alive.
In the twilight's embrace, let laughter abound,
For joy in the dark is where fun can be found!

Shimmering Silhouettes

In shadows they shimmer, a giggling sight,
Dancing like fireflies in the night.
Wobbling and wobbling, they wave around,
Creating a buzz, a delightful sound.

They play peek-a-boo with the fading sun,
Oh, the shenanigans! Oh, what fun!
Twisting and turning, they steal the show,
With a hint of sparkle, ready to glow.

A nudge here, a jive there, all in good cheer,
Friendships are forged when the end draws near.
In a flicker of light, a chuckle ensues,
These shimmering figures share silly views.

So dance with abandon, let laughter outshine,
For in the twilight, all secrets entwine.
With whimsical joy, let's make this a night,
Of shimmering silhouettes, gleaming so bright!

A Symphony of Glow

With twinkling giggles, they shimmer and spin,
A symphony of glow where fun begins.
Dressed in mischief, they jingle with cheer,
Creating a melody all can hear.

Each bob and each sway tells tales of delight,
As shadows play tricks in the softening light.
A chorus of laughter, a ballet so grand,
These quirky little gems take their stand.

Let's march to the rhythm, oh what a sight!
In harmony's laughter, everything feels right.
With a wink and a wiggle, they take the stage,
A jubilant dance, they set the world ablaze.

So join in the fun, let your heart swell,
In this symphony of glow, all is well.
For in every sparkle, joy takes its flight,
As we celebrate life in the fading light!

Celestial Auras in Hushed Night

In a world of stars that gleam,
Comedy flows like a wild dream.
Behold the gems that sway and sway,
Laughing softly at the end of day.

Charming lights that waltz with glee,
Mischief wrapped in mystery.
They twinkle like eyes on the prowl,
Ready to giggle, ready to howl.

The sky wears laughter, quite the sight,
As dainty treasures catch the light.
They toss their heads, all in jest,
"Look at us, we're truly best!"

Dear friends of night, so light and spry,
They shimmer, sparkle, and then fly.
In the hush, they play their tune,
Tickling the laughter of the moon.

Adornments Whispering to the Moon.

Oh trinkets dancing in the breeze,
Stirring up a fit of tease.
A jingle here, a jangle there,
As sunshine bids the day to spare.

The moonbeam giggles in delight,
Watching ornaments take flight.
OH! How they wiggle, shimmy, and twirl,
Like cheeky sprites that spin and whirl.

"Oh darlings, are we fancy enough?
Or should we wear the silly stuff?"
Adornments chat as night descends,
Gleeful whispers, mischievous friends.

They call the stars to join the fun,
Pulling pranks till the night is done.
In the shade of an evening's cue,
Shiny secrets found anew.

Whispers of Dusk

As daylight nods and whispers low,
Funny glints start to show.
Tiny treasures in a frolicsome race,
Playing hide and seek in a cozy space.

Ah! The laughter of the evening mist,
Each sparkle winks, none can resist.
They giggle and hide, so spry and bright,
Bringing mischief to the gentle night.

"Who wore it best?" the shadows quip,
As charms begin their giddy trip.
Twirling high in a festive spree,
Nighttime revelry, oh what glee!

In twilight's grasp of soft embrace,
Laughter dances all over the place.
Bright little wonders with tales to share,
Whisking us off to dreamland's lair.

Glimmers of Dusk

The sky dons its playful attire,
As charms laugh, never tire.
With a twinkle here and a glimmer there,
Joking stars in a cosmic affair.

"We're the jesters of the night!"
They laugh and tease in pure delight.
Swinging on silver threads of fate,
Making dusk their stage, oh how they skate!

"Let's spin in circles, make a show!
Bounce around with all we know!"
Each tiny gem, a merry sprite,
Shining brighter as they unite.

In the fading light, a jolly band,
Creating joy from every strand.
Sidle close, the night is young,
With whispers sweet and songs unsung.

Lattice of Light

In the moon's soft chuckle, gems start to sway,
A dance of whimsy, come out to play.
Crickets chirp secrets in the night air,
While glittering friends hang without a care.

A quirky parade of colors on display,
They twirl with laughter, in a stylish ballet.
Swaying like leaves in a light breeze,
Who knew this fun could come so easy?

Frogs make a chorus, join in on the fun,
Under the stars, resolution undone.
The sky bursts with laughter, cheeky and bright,
As gems wink and giggle in soft golden light.

With each little jingle, secrets untold,
A story of mischief begins to unfold.
Underneath the glow, let humor entwine,
In this lattice of laughter, we sip on moonshine.

Glistening Whispers

In the shadows where sparkles begin to play,
Giggles erupt as stars give way.
A mischievous glimmer, lighting the scene,
Winking and nodding, as bright as can be.

Chirpy little voices float through the air,
Telling tall tales of a magical fair.
With a snicker and wink, they dance 'round the tree,
Spreading sweet chaos so joyfully free.

While fireflies mock with their twinkling show,
Even the flowers can't help but glow.
A scene full of laughter, oh what a sight,
Whispers of glistening in the cool night.

Each sparkle a giggle, a laugh in the dark,
Creating a ruckus, igniting a spark.
In this shimmering frolic, we all take part,
Glistening whispers that tickle the heart.

Twilight Adorned

As shadows stretch and the light starts to fade,
The night's little jesters dance, unafraid.
With flashes of color that bubble and pop,
In a world upside down, they all skip and hop.

With glee like a child, in the dim evening blue,
They spin spun stories, all lively and new.
A festival of whimsy unfolds in delight,
As giggles of stardust escape into night.

A jingle, a jangle, what mischief they share,
As laughter unfolds in the cool evening air.
Each moment a delight, a toe-tapping song,
Twilight adorned, where we all can belong.

So let's twirl in the twilight, in pure revelry,
With a flick and a twist, come and dance with me.
For in every shimmer, joy is reborn,
In this twilight playground, we are never forlorn.

Celestial Elegance

Beneath a blanket of stars, the fun begins,
Where laughter resonates and light whimsically spins.
With dazzling displays that dazzle the eye,
They twist like a comet through the darkening sky.

Marshmallow dreams float on beams of pure glow,
Each twinkle a wink, cheerful, aglow.
Crickets conspire, each chirp a delight,
Encouraging mischief throughout the night.

With every shimmery hop, a burst of glee,
As shadows perform an elaborate spree.
In this celestial charm, laughter's our guide,
On this whimsical journey, we take a wild ride.

So gather your friends for this festival bright,
In the celestial elegance, everything's light.
With a giggle or two and a sparkle or three,
Let's sail through the stars, oh joyous and free!

Radiance in the Gloom

In the dim light, they shimmer bright,
A dance of sparkles, what a sight.
Laughing shadows tease and play,
As we stumble on our way.

Glimmers wink from frumpy ears,
Turning heads, igniting cheers.
Who knew fashion could be fun?
In this dark, we've just begun!

Giant hoops like hula hoops,
Wobbling 'round like silly troops.
Under stars that start to fade,
We've made our own charade!

A little vintage, a dash of flair,
Next to us, the moon's aware.
Amidst the giggles, shy and spry,
Who needs sunlight? We're flying high!

Enshrined in Shadows

Caught in the night, a glint like glee,
Mischief wrapped in sparkly spree.
Poking fun, we twirl and sway,
As shadows dance, we laugh and play.

An odd pair, mismatched for sure,
Those tangled threads, a fashion lure.
Twisting hoops like licorice loops,
Who knew we'd look like silly stoops?

Glistening gems on flopping lobes,
Adding flair to our wobbly robes.
If laughter's gold, we're rich tonight,
In this chaos, everything's bright!

We're echoes of joy, unabashedly grand,
With every twinkle, let's take a stand.
In shadows where lunacy thrives,
We adorn the night with giggly lives!

Fading Echoes

In dusk's embrace, the twinkles fade,
But our laughter hovers, never strayed.
From silly blunders, style's reborn,
Each gleaming pearl becomes our thorn.

Who knew these trinkets could bring such cheer?
With every jingle, we hold them near.
Swapping stories beneath the stars,
As we trip over our own bizarre.

With rhinestones that sparkle and shimmer low,
Goofy glam is the way we flow.
We trade our tales for a chance to shine,
In fading echoes, we're truly divine!

While shadows stretch and stars collide,
We wear our joys like a silly pride.
In this night, mischief aligns,
With fading echoes, our humor shines!

Adorned in Mystery

With a dash of flair, and a jingle jive,
We wear our oddities, fabulously alive.
In whispers of dusk, our laughter hides,
As we prance around on these goofy rides.

A touch of glimmer, a pinch of fun,
Our crazy styles weigh a ton!
Mixing patterns, colors collide,
In this mad world, we take a stride.

Who cares if things don't quite match?
That's the essence, we'll happily catch!
Even tangles turn into trends,
In mysterious ways, our humor blends!

As the night falls with its gentle tease,
We're adorned in laughter, a night that frees.
Magic unfolds in our sparkling ruckus,
In this mystery, we find our focus!

Glistening Dreams

In the night where oddities dwell,
Bobbing beads dance, they're under a spell.
They giggle and jingle in delight,
As they spin tales of the moonlight.

A quirky trio with glittering flair,
Whispering secrets, they play without care.
On mischievous wind, they float and glide,
Stealing the spotlight, they cannot hide.

Beneath the stars, they twinkle and sway,
Jokes unfold in a dazzling display.
Who knew that beads could jest and tease?
In their shimmering world, they do as they please.

So, let the night wear its fanciest sights,
With whimsical dreams and laughter in flights.
A little sparkle can brighten the gloom,
As we dance with our dreams, creating a boom.

Echoes Beneath the Stars

In the still of night, laughter erupts,
Amidst sparkly gems, the joy interrupts.
With chimes of mischief, they bounce all around,
Making every moment a giggling sound.

Starry beings, they wiggle and tease,
Spinning tales on a playful breeze.
A pop of color, a dash of glee,
Amusing each other with comical spree.

Beneath the moon's gaze, their stories unfold,
Whimsical whispers wrapped in pure gold.
They jive and jangle, a wacky display,
Stars beaming back as they humorously play.

Bringing joy to the radiant night,
These giggling jewels twinkle delight.
In every chortle, in every bright beam,
Life is just better – a shared, lively dream.

Adornments of the Evening

In this bustling night, beads burst with cheer,
Jingling in rhythm, they hold us near.
Like little sprites, they sparkle and prance,
In hilarious moments, they take a stance.

Fashioned for fun, they dangle with glee,
Shouting out joy for the world to see.
Twirling around like butterflies in flight,
Adding laughter, oh what a sight!

Their playful antics, like a farcical show,
Make us all lighten and toss worries below.
A misfit band beneath the night sky,
Leaving us grinning as they flit by.

With a crinkle of laughter, they steal the scene,
Adornments of joy, like we've never seen.
So let's raise a toast to the whimsical crew,
For making the night feel fresh and new!

Radiant Reflections

A twinkle here, a shimmer there,
Radiant beads in electric air.
They giggle and wink, causing a stir,
As the night wraps us in its cozy purr.

They skip like children with no care in sight,
Making shadows dance in the pale moonlight.
A comical bunch with tales to tell,
Their playful hi-jinks cast a bright spell.

Glancing in mirrors, they sparkle in fun,
Each jest a reflection, a burst of the sun.
Their laughter rings out in glorious tones,
As they prance around like silly bones.

Twilight smiles as the night sways along,
To a quirky beat, a luminous song.
Let's join the revel, let laughter be king,
As twinkling treasures dance and sing.

Celestial Drops of Evening Grace

As day gives way to dusk's embrace,
A pair of sparkles starts to race.
They twirl in glee, so full of cheer,
Daring the stars to join them here.

With a wink, they flip and slide,
Like playful cheeks in evening's tide.
Their laughter rings through fading light,
As shadows dance, they feel so right.

They gossip 'bout the moon's new phase,
And chuckle loud in twilight's haze.
In whispered tones, they share a joke,
These shiny gems, with sparkle's poke.

So let them swirl in gentle winds,
As night begins, the fun transcends.
For in this dance of evening's grace,
The world finds joy in their embrace.

Nightfall's Swaying Trinkets

When day retreats and evening thrives,
Two trinkets leap, they come alive.
They swing and sway in vibrant show,
A comedic duo, stealing glow.

With every glimmer, they recite,
The story of a silly fight.
One teased the moon, calling it pale,
While the other laughed and began to wail.

Through playful jingles, round they go,
In a swirling twilight, soft and slow.
In ranks of stars, they find their mates,
And dance together, dodging fates.

They countdown seconds to the night,
With ticklish giggles, pure delight.
These trinkets sway and steal the scene,
In nightfall's embrace, oh what a dream!

Luminous Hoops Under an Indigo Sky

In indigo skies, two hoops gleam bright,
Taking garden strolls in soft moonlight.
With each little twirl, they tell their tales,
Of wild chases with magical snails.

They joke about the stars' lost spark,
And reenact a race 'til it's dark.
With gentle spins, they twinkle and sway,
Creating laughter that won't decay.

As night calls forth its cosmic crew,
These luminous orbs bid adieu.
With a skip and a hop, they grasp the breeze,
Turning twilight to a glorious tease.

Through flickers of joy, they play and prance,
Eager to join the night's grand dance.
Their humor shines, a beacon to see,
In the vastness of night, they're wild and free.

The Dance of Silver Reflections

Silver sparks in the evening's glow,
Reflecting giggles like soft pillows.
In their shimmering rhythm, they light the way,
Always with a wink, come what may.

They leap across dark, just like a rhyme,
Conducting mischief through the night's chime.
With every twist, a chuckle escapes,
As they spin in circles, pulling funny shapes.

Glancing at the stars, they take a chance,
Inviting the moon to join their dance.
With a twirl and a flap, they sway on high,
Creating ripples as dreams pass by.

So let them shine as day's last thread,
In silver reflections where laughter's led.
For through their frolic, the night does sing,
A comical chase, to joy they cling.

Glistening Orbs at Dusk

As the sun dips low and shadows play,
Little bulbs of joy start their ballet.
Hopping on lobes like a party parade,
They jingle and jive, never afraid.

Bright sparkles teasing a curious gaze,
Dancing like fireflies in a maze.
Who knew such trinkets could steal the show?
A comical sight, putting on a glow!

Whispering Gems Beneath the Stars

In the starlight's glow, a giggle is found,
Bling blinks and winks, making quite the sound.
Each little bauble with a secret to share,
They gossip of mischief, floating in air.

As night draws near, they form a cheer,
Whispering tales that only they hear.
Tiny chums so jolly and bright,
Swaying together in whimsical flight.

Moonlit Charms of Silhouette

With a gleam of the night, they begin to sway,
Casting silly shadows that dance in play.
On the head of a clown or the ear of a dog,
Making all passersby stop and just gawk.

Laughter erupts at their comical stance,
Moonlit mischief leads to a dance.
Oh what a sight, so foolish and light,
These charms in silhouette bring pure delight!

Shimmering Adornments in the Shadow

Glittering glitterbugs sitting with flair,
Caught in a snapshot, a performer's dare.
They spin and they twirl in a shadowy stage,
Drawing in laughter from all of their age.

In the twilight's embrace, they plot and they plan,
To turn every frown into a bright span.
With a shimmer and shake, they wink and they tease,
These curls of mischief make hearts feel at ease.

Secrets of the Night Adorned

In the dark, they sway and dangle,
Like little fish in a playful tangle.
Whispers of glimmer, a sly little tease,
Making me giggle with all of their ease.

They jump and jive under the moon's soft beams,
Making me ponder and plotting my dreams.
With every shimmer, a joke they tell,
Laughing together, oh, do they do well!

Hiding secrets in each gleaming loop,
Telling tales of a whimsical group.
Their chuckles resound, light as a feather,
Creating a dance in the nocturnal weather.

When night descends, chaos takes flight,
With sparkles that giggle with pure delight.
So raise a toast to these charming charms,
For every twinkle carries their larks!

Midnight Melodies of Beads

When the world zips off to sleepy land,
Beads start their band, you won't believe how they stand.
Strumming the night with songs of delight,
Making the moon jealous, oh, what a sight!

They roll and they roll, from table to floor,
Singing in harmony—who could ask for more?
Jingle and jangle, in rhythmic delight,
The beads have a party that lasts through the night.

With every little hop, they chuckle and cheer,
Reminding the stars that laughter is near.
Sounds of the night, woven in lace,
This bead band knows how to set the pace!

So if you wander when the hour is late,
Join the parade, don't miss out—don't wait!
For midnight melodies echo and play,
With joyous little beads dancing away!

Serenity in Silhouette Sparkles

In shadows, they shimmer, as mischief unfolds,
Sparkles like giggles, oh, the stories they told.
Striding through glances, with elegance swirled,
Bringing a grin to the stillness of the world.

Each twinkling dance, they prance with delight,
Making us chuckle, igniting the night.
They beckon the stars with their delicate charms,
Whispering secrets of hushed, funny qualms.

As they sway in the breeze, laughter ignites,
Creating a ruckus amidst calming nights.
In quiet repose, they jest and they tease,
Wrapped in the silliness of whimsical ease.

So if you see outlines that sparkle and dance,
Do chuckle aloud, give laughter a chance.
Let shadows unearth their giggles and glee,
For serenity comes where the fun is carefree!

The Allure of Dusk's Embrace

As the sun yawns wide, it wears a soft grin,
Dusk tugs at the day, a playful spin.
With a wink in the dark, chaos does bloom,
Mischief emerges from shadowy gloom.

Glimmers dance like fireflies, such a delight,
A comedy show under the soft star light.
With stories of silly from dusk until dawn,
They twinkle and jive, a whimsical song.

A laughter parade, oh, how they collide,
With every new glimmer, they dance and they hide.
In the comforting arms of the night's gentle face,
Mirth and joy merge in dusk's warm embrace.

So, when evening falls, don't forget to gaze,
At the sparkles and giggles that dance in a maze.
For the allure is real, and the fun never tires,
In the embrace of the dusk, where the laughter inspires!

Radiant Pendants in dusky Hues

In the evening glow, they dance with glee,
Hanging like fruit from a wild cherry tree.
A wink from the moon, a giggle from stars,
They jingle and jive like little poptarts.

Each sway tells a joke, a story to share,
These glimmering charms with flair, do they care?
A clumsy flutter, a twinkle, a grin,
As they saunter about, letting fashion win.

In the soft, fading light, their secrets unfurl,
With every raucous laugh, they twirl, twirl, twirl!
Who knew such baubles could be this much fun?
A quirky parade when the day is done.

So here's to the night, may it sparkle and shine,
With radiant baubles, oh isn't life fine!
They seem to delight in the chaos they weave,
Playful and bright, just like tricks up their sleeves.

Starlit Jewels on Velvet Ears

Perched on soft lobes, they shine so bright,
Like fireflies caught in a game of the night.
Each glint a giggle, each sway a cheer,
As whispers of mischief linger so near.

Could it be magic or just good old luck?
These starlit wonders bring giggles unstuck.
When friends come around, they start a small brawl,
To snatch them and flaunt them, it's laughter for all.

With a gentle tug, they wiggle and sway,
As if they have something fun to say.
"Hey you! Look at us, we're the life of the show!
Come join our waltz; it's your turn to glow!"

So revel in jewels that whisper and tease,
On ears of velvet, they aim to please.
In this huddle of sparkle, we party all night,
With starlit adornments, everything feels right.

Ethereal Chimes of the Dimming Light

As daylight bids farewell, they start to hum,
A melody playful, a sweet little drum.
Chimes of delight in the dusk they reveal,
Echoes of laughter that shimmy and squeal.

Tickling the breeze, they jingle with flair,
'Tis a hilarious circus, with not a care.
"Who's the funniest?" they giggle in rhyme,
They bounce and they bounce, a theatrical mime.

The night wears its jewels, a whimsical show,
With echoes of laughter that dance to and fro.
Chimes in the twilight, aren't they a sight?
Unwrap the joy, spread the giggles tonight!

To those who adorn the ear with such grace,
Let's celebrate whimsy, a merry embrace!
In the festival of dusk, let the laughter ignite,
With chimes of delight, we float through the night.

Nocturnal Whispers of Fashion

In shadows they shimmer, a quirky delight,
Nocturnal whispers, oh what a sight!
Strange tales they tell as they jostle around,
In styles unpredictable, beauty abounds.

"Wear me this way, or mayhaps like a crown?"
Each piece with personality abounds!
A silly parade of colors and spark,
Poking and prodding till they leave their mark.

In giggles they frolic, as if in a race,
Strutting their stuff with such humor and grace.
"Aren't we the best? Who knew we could shine?"
They tease and they laugh while we sip on our wine.

So let's twirl in fashion, with whimsical flair,
With nocturnal whispers floating in air.
Life's too short to be serious, right?
So let's wear our laughter, in the still of the night!

Shimmering Enchantment

Tiny baubles twinkle and sway,
Hang on lobes like they're on a holiday.
Why do they dance? Is it sheer delight?
Or are they just trying to take flight?

A lady laughs, her grin quite wide,
As her sparkly gems try to hide.
"Did they just wink?" one friend inquires,
"Or are they plotting little liar fires?"

Each glint a secret, a comic plot,
Whispering tales to what we forgot.
Shining bright with mischief's cue,
Those lovely gems have much to do!

At dusk they gather, a silly crew,
Stirring up tales of what they knew.
In this laughter, let's join the spree,
For friendship shines, just wait and see!

Secrets of the Nocturnal

In shadows, they giggle and glow,
Mysteries lurking in every throw.
Did you see that one dart? What a tease!
Under the moon, like mischievous bees!

Plots are brewing in the dim-lit air,
Ears adorned with joy, never a care.
A nod, a wink, a jolly song,
These hidden treasures just can't be wrong!

Glimmering whispers of night's parade,
Each sparkling hint of a playful charade.
A sudden twirl could make you fall,
For such small beads, they're quite the ball!

Ah! The secrets that night will hold,
With every chime, the stories unfold.
Laughing voices in an endless jest,
Who knew that gems could be so blessed?

Moonlit Trinkets

What's that sparkling in the night?
Hold on tight, it's quite a sight!
Dancing round in storms of glee,
These tiny charms are wild and free!

With every jiggle, they make a sound,
A comic retort from all around.
"Look at me!" they seem to shout,
As they whizz and swirl without a doubt!

On lazy evenings, they join the fray,
Playing hide and seek in a crazy way.
"I found the red one! Have you seen blue?"
These moonlit trinkets are good at peek-a-boo!

Who knew such fun could be had,
With delicate things that make us glad?
Together they twinkle, a sparkly dream,
In the night, they're part of the gleam!

The Veil of Evening Glow

Beneath a veil of shimmer and shine,
Frolicsome bits make the night divine.
"Are they alive?" one child will ask,
As gems chuckle, wearing their mask.

With a flicker here and a dash there,
They glide and twirl through the fresh air.
In the moon's glow, they play their part,
Filling each moment with quirky art!

A twinkling jest from ear to ear,
Setting the stage with giggles near.
Bedecked in charms, oh what a view,
Even the stars are joining too!

In this nightly escapade, so sweet,
The universe bends to their beat.
Laughter echoes beneath the sky,
Unruly trinkets making time fly!

Evening's Gentle Touch

The sun has packed its bags, you see,
As shadows dance and giggles flee.
A moth just tried to steal my snack,
I watch it wobble, then attack!

The breeze brings whispers, secrets told,
Of cats who think they're brave and bold.
A frog joins in, a croaking song,
I laugh so hard; this night feels long!

The stars all wink as if to tease,
A sneaky bat, who moves with ease.
I trip on grass, it's quite a show,
A tumble there, but still I glow!

The moon, a jester in the sky,
Throws shadows that just seem to fly.
With every twist and turn I take,
The night's a laugh, make no mistake!

Whims of the Night

With dusk, the playful spirits roam,
A raccoon thinks it found a home.
It dives into a trash can's glee,
While laughing light, it's just like me!

In corners dim, the crickets sing,
Of tiresome days and silly things.
I join their choir, harmonize,
While owls watch with their big surprise!

The wind, it whispers, "Can you dare?"
To dance with shadows in the air.
I prance around, a silly show,
In moonlight's glow, I steal the show!

A lizard darts; it zips right by,
While stars start blinking in the sky.
What fun it is to play at night,
With giggles shared and pure delight!

Veils of Evening Grace

As twilight drapes a velvet sheet,
The world turns soft, a cozy treat.
But oh! What's that? A prankster breeze,
A feathered hat? Now that's a tease!

The shadows stretch, they leap and twirl,
A squirrel now joins; what a whirl!
He hops and skips on tiny feet,
With every bound, it's quite a feat!

The moon, it snickers, casts a glare,
As I trip over my own hair.
At dusk, we smile, we laugh and play,
The night's a friend, come what may!

Frogs leap like dancers in the sun,
On lily pads, they have such fun.
And with a wink, the stars align,
To share a giggle, oh so fine!

Luminous Memories

With night's embrace, the fun unfolds,
A comet's tail, a tale retold.
A wobbly chair, so full of squeaks,
Hosts silly secrets, giggly peaks!

The dancing lights, they float and spin,
As fireflies play, my head's in a din.
In twinkling chaos, my heart will race,
With every flicker, a cheeky grace!

The moonlight spills like iced up tea,
While shadows frolic, wild and free.
I chase the giggles floating by,
In luminous joy beneath the sky!

Oh, what a night, so bright, so bold,
With laughter shared, the tales retold.
In every heart, a memory glows,
As the funny magic of twilight flows!

A Soft Embrace of Metal

In the dark, they twinkle tight,
Hiding secrets, oh what a sight!
Fashioned from dreams and giggles small,
Jokes on the floor from their fall.

They swing like pendulums, so bold,
Once lost, now found, a tale to be told.
A gentle jingle, a joyful dance,
Who knew they'd hold such a chance?

Round and shiny, a comical spree,
They whisper softly, 'Look at me!'
In the shadows, they laugh and tease,
In a world where nonsense aims to please.

A hiccup here, a tumble there,
Time for fun, who has a care?
They bring a chuckle, a playful glee,
In the twilight, they hold the key.

Twinkling Beauties

They sparkle like stars in a canteen,
Making faces, oh what a scene!
Dancing around like fireflies bright,
Creating chaos in the night.

Rattling round with a cheeky chime,
Losing track of space and time,
They're mischief-makers in disguise,
Popping up with joke-filled eyes.

Round and plump, they twist and spin,
Each one a story, where to begin?
Laughter bubbles in every ear,
As they whisper, 'We're happy here!'

A clang, a clink, a shiny flare,
Making moments we love to share,
With every blink, they steal the show,
In the twilight's glow, oh how they flow!

The Echoing Gleam

Glinting mischief, who could resist?
A pot of gold, they seem so kissed.
Every wobble a sound, so bright,
  Chirping joy in the dim twilight.

They jingle with laughter, a joyous sound,
Rolling 'round, they leap off the ground.
Caught mid-laugh, with stories to tell,
  Shining like secrets in a wishing well.

Chasing shadows, they bounce and sway,
  In their playful, whimsical way.
Every little shimmer, a chance to play,
  Creating comedy, come what may.

With a wink and a jig, they flaunt their fame,
  Bringing joy in a sparkling game.
A whimsical treasure, they steal the light,
  In the chuckling chaos of the night.

Dusk's Delicate Fashion

In the twilight, mischief made,
A cloak of fun in which they trade.
Dressed in giggles, a comical flair,
What a sight to make you stare.

Fashionable yet full of cheer,
Tickling thoughts when they appear.
Frivolous antics, a playful tease,
Filling the night with joyous ease.

A flash of silver, a twist of fate,
Wobbling around, but never late.
Chasing shadows, igniting laughs,
While moonlight points at their crazy paths.

As dusk descends and night does call,
There's laughter echoing above it all.
In their reflection, pure delight blooms,
Where fun collides in whispered tunes.

Silken Gleams of the Night

In the dark, they sway and twirl,
Like disco balls in a mystical whirl.
A flash here, a sparkle there,
Who knew pearls could do the cha-cha in midair?

A tap on the shoulder, a gleeful shout,
'What's that shiny thing hanging out?'
With a giggle, I whisper, 'A charm so bright,'
Or perhaps it's just my snack from last night!

Laughter around as they jingle away,
Dancing through shadows like bright playful rays.
Each figure of fun with its little surprise,
Like tiny clowns wearing disguise!

In the glimmering glow, let antics unfold,
Stories of mischief in twinkles retold.
As night takes its bow, what a curious sight,
The party's just started, oh what a delight!

The Allure of Soft Glows

Underneath the moon, they bounce and play,
Chatting with stars, come what may.
With a wink, they signal, 'Join the show!'
Oh, those tiny winks put on a glow!

Flickers and flashes, oh what a scene,
Wobbling like jellybeans, ever so keen.
Catch me if you can, they tease and dance,
In the night's spotlight, they haven't a chance!

From the shadows, I hear their cheer,
Whispers of joy that tickle the ear.
"Is that a magician?" I chuckle with glee,
Or just shiny gems playing tricks on me?

With borrowed light, they laugh and gleam,
Adventures in dusk like a whimsical dream.
As the curtain drops, they bid adieu,
Leaving a trail of laughter anew!

Glimmers of the Ethereal

Floating about, in the cool night air,
Little gems prancing without a care.
"Are you mine?" they ask with a silver grin,
I reply with a wink, "Only if you spin!"

In the corner, they whisper and tease,
'Come play with us, we promise to please!'
Each gleam a promise of silly delight,
Who knew bling could be such a fright?

Off they go, like stars in a race,
Chasing fireflies, a jubilant chase.
"I can outshine you!" they giggle and jest,
Oh love, what a game, it's all for the best!

As night settles in with a soft melodic hum,
The laughter continues, oh what fun!
With starlit tales twinkling bright,
In the warm embrace of shimmering night!

Dabbles of Light in Darkness

In the dim, they glisten, playfully bright,
Like fireflies lost in a whimsical flight.
"What's that shimmer?" the shadows implore,
A symphony of chuckles, forever more!

Bumping and bouncing with a jolly delight,
Fleeting and funny in the cloak of night.
Dancing around with a twirl and a leap,
Not a care in the world, not a secret to keep!

With each glint, a riddle pops up,
"Is it magic, or just a hiccup?"
With a belly laugh, they sway and spin,
Making me wonder how they fit in!

As the moonlight wanes, the fun never ends,
Every flicker a story that bends and blends.
In this dance of shadows, joy takes its flight,
Dabbles of laughter, oh what a sight!

Dusk's Glistening Artistry

As shadows stretch and light takes flight,
A pair of shiny baubles laugh in the night.
They jingle like chimes in the warm evening air,
Whispering secrets, without a care.

But one's a bit crooked, it's got a wild flair,
While the other just sways like it's caught unaware.
They peek from a purse, oh what a delight,
Ready to party under the moonlight!

With glimmers of gold and sparkles of glass,
They wink at the stars, daring them to pass.
In the dance of the dusk, they're the life of the show,
Making even the cacti join in the glow!

So bring on the laughter, the jokes, and the cheer,
These sparkling fibs spread joy far and near.
Adorn yourself silly, wear fun to the core,
Life is too short to be a total bore!

Fragments of Radiance

In the corner shop, the deals are quite grand,
A pair of odd trinkets, oh, isn't that planned?
One's shaped like a taco, the other a cat,
Worn with a grin, they're where it's at!

Underneath streetlights, they flicker and gleam,
Inviting the giggles, igniting the dream.
Fashion faux pas? Not in our book,
As we strut with style, take a second look!

With laughter surrounding each unique display,
These odd little jewels lead the dance, come what may.
Clicking together, they clash with such flair,
Spreading a joy that hangs in the air!

So grab your odd pieces, don't be shy,
Wear them with spirit, let your heart fly.
In fragments of radiance, we shine so bright,
Navigating the dusk with pure delight!

Starry Embellishments

Twinkly things, beneath a soft glow,
Dangled and dangled, oh where will they go?
A nighttime adventure for all to behold,
In jokes and in laughter, our tales unfold.

Each sparkly charm tells a tale of its own,
From disco to dinner, they shiver and moan.
A butterfly flutters but loses one side,
While the other keeps dancing, a twinkling guide!

As friends gather 'round with a bubbly cheer,
Their tricks and their sparkles create quite the sphere.
With mismatched colors, they giggle and fight,
Saying, "Who needs matching? We shine just right!"

So raise up a toast to embellishments bright,
Cherish the laughter that fills up the night.
With starry bits dancing, be wild and be free,
Let's wear our oddities, just you and me!

The Subtle Art of Adornment

In a world full of chaos, we spice it with glee,
With snippets of sparkle, just wait and see.
A pair of bananas, who thought they'd wear gold?
In the frolicsome twilight, be brave and be bold!

Twirling in laughter, they dangle and swing,
Creating a vibe that makes hearts take wing.
When the moon rises up, they tap on the glass,
Silly little jewelry, letting time pass!

So mix up the colors, the shine and the flair,
The subtle art's giggles, floating through air.
With each little winkle, our spirits ignite,
Let's craft our own twinkles; we'll conquer the night!

Ah, the joy of the silly, let's start a new trend,
With laughter as treasures, this night will not end.
From trinkets to giggles, we dance to the fun,
In the soft, swaying twilight, we've only begun!

Enchanted Reflections of Fading Light

In the hush of dusk's parade,
A sparkly debate is displayed.
Glitter bugs dance on the wire,
While shadows giggle and conspire.

Jewel thieves on the watchful prowl,
Sneak around like a grinning owl.
They snatch the glint and make it sing,
A harmonized chime—a vibrant fling!

A ladybird dons a shiny crown,
With polka dots, she's the talk of the town.
Raccoons wear bling, it's quite absurd,
Chasing after dreams, have you heard?

Night's gown sparkles, we can't resist,
A comical twist in a jewel-studded tryst.
Laughter echoed, reflections shine bright,
In twilight's embrace, such pure delight!

Mystical Luminance of Evening Tryst

A squirrel with bling, quite a sight,
Stealing snacks under the neon light.
With races spun in whirlwinds of fun,
Who knew twilight could be so undone?

The stars wink down with a cheeky smile,
As shadows jiggle, making us stay awhile.
A mischief of mice with acorn charms,
Throw a soiree that wins hearts and warms.

Whispers of breezes, tickling the air,
Swaying the fauna in elegant flair.
The moon wobbles with laughter too,
As glittery tales start to accrue!

Every rustle tells stories, take note,
As twilight flirts in a glowing coat.
In this mystic dance, nothing feels amiss,
Save for the hiccups and the starry bliss!

The Last Light of Adorned Sophistication

Gems tucked in the bushy tail of a fox,
As laughter rings through the midnight rocks.
Glamorous owls with their spectacles bright,
Debate who's the richest in shimmering light.

Fiddlesticks and flower crowns in tow,
Let's twirl under stars in twilight's glow.
A bashful badger takes a bow,
While birds chirp banter without a row.

The raccoon brigade with plundered treats,
Stoops and sneaks down on mischievous fleets.
In a twinkling vista, with mirth piled high,
Join the fable of twinkling sky!

When the moon rolls in, with elegance so rare,
Sassy sprites flaunt their gala flair.
In the last light, we all abide,
With laughs that dance and bubbly pride!

Silvescent Secrets of the Gloaming

At the edge of day, creatures conspire,
A platypus dashing, with endless desire.
Ocean of grass sways with delight,
As secrets shimmer and twinkle at night.

Elves with charms and a paintbrush too,
Create twinkling art—who knew they could do?
Fireflies play tag, in a sparkling race,
While murmurs of magic fill up the space.

Tiny frogs in top hats convene,
Discussing the tales of the pure and obscene.
With laughter like ripples in twilight so clear,
They croak out joy, everyone cheer!

As daylight winks, the world closes shop,
Admired gems on critters—hop, hop, hop!
Secrets of evening, so playful, so grand,
In silly river tales that wave their hands!

www.ingramcontent.com/pod-product-compliance
Lightning Source LLC
Chambersburg PA
CBHW060125230426
43661CB00003B/334